I0171645

Seals, Trumpets and Vials

and how they culminate on Jewish New Year in 2012

Seals, Trumpets and Vials
and how they culminate on
Jewish New Year in 2012
Copyright © 2009 Eve Clarity

All rights reserved. No part of this publication may be reproduced except for brief quotations in printed reviews without the prior permission of the author.

All Scripture quotations are from the American King James Version of the Holy Bible which is in the public domain. Bold lettering and underlining has been added in the text for emphasis.

ISBN 978-1-931203-16-6

Published by Inspired Idea

Inspired Idea
Innovative Christ-Centered Learning

For more information, go to
http://www.kneelingmedia.org/AwakeBride/
The complete book is available at amazon.com
and http://stores.lulu.com/awakebride

TABLE OF CONTENTS

Page #

Introduction   i

God's Team and Satan's Team   9

Book of Revelation   9

Scroll with the Seven Seals: Marriage Contract   10

    Jesus Purchased the Right to Open It   11

Four Horsemen (Seals #1-4)   14

What Event Starts 3 1/2 Year Clock?   18

First Four Trumpets and Vials   21

5th Trumpet and Vial   22

5th Seal (Martyrs)   23

6th Vial and Trumpet (Armegeddon)   24

6th Seal   26

Signs Immediately Before Christ's 2nd Coming   28

    7th Vial   29

    7th Seal   29

    7th Trumpet   30

King Jesus Returns and Fights and Reigns   30

Order and Timing of Seals, Trumpets and Vials   33

Summary   33

Great Tribulation Time-Line of Revelation chart   36

Introduction

This booklet will present the Scriptures regarding the Seals, Trumpets, and Vials described by John, the apostle, in the book of Revelation. It is actually a chapter from my book titled, *Awake, Bride,* which contains the research for these conclusions. In that book I go into detail regarding the Hebrew feasts and calendar, the historical fulfillments of prophecies in Daniel 2, 9 and 11 and Ezekiel 38-39, and the prophecies of the year of Christ's second coming as 2012 from Daniel 8 and 12. It presents a clear case for a post-tribulation resurrection and rapture at Christ's second coming, and how Jesus provided us the day and the time of His arrival in Matthew 24-25 (Jewish New Year at midnight).

The prophecies in Daniel correctly predict the year of Christ's first coming as well as His second. Jesus fulfilled the Spring Feasts during His first coming; He will fulfill the Fall Feasts during His second coming. The first Fall Feast is Jewish New Year (Rosh Hashanah) which occurs on a new moon which could only be established by the Sanhedrin in Jesus' time, so it was the only feast that the day was unknown until it was announced. If you were to ask any betrothed Jewish man of Jesus' time, "When is the date of your wedding?" He would respond, "No one knows the day or the hour, except my father." The groom could not fetch his bride until his father deemed the groom had completed construction of the bridal chamber. In Matthew 25 Jesus tells the parable of the ten virgins and the groom who arrives at midnight. My conclusion is that scripture points to September 16, 2012 as the date of Christ's second coming.

To Christian Readers, my intended audience:

God said, "*Call to me, and I will answer you, and show you great and mighty things, which you know not*" (Jeremiah 33:3). The testimony of Jesus is the spirit of prophecy (Rev. 19:10c, 13b); so we come to worship God as we study His Word, and call to Him for revelation. I encourage you to read the book of Revelation, which is a blessing all its own, and to ask God to give you wisdom.

And the very God of peace sanctify you wholly; and I pray God your whole spirit and soul and body be preserved blameless to the coming of our Lord Jesus Christ. (1 Thessalonians 5:23)

To Muslim Readers:

Just as Islam has two main branches of Sunni and Shia, and many other sects besides; so Christianity has Catholicism and Protestantism with hundreds of various denominations. I am not Catholic and I don't worship Mary. The triune God I worship is the Father and His Son, Jesus, and His Holy Spirit. God, the Father, did not have sex with Mary. She was a virgin who miraculously gave birth to Jesus. Jesus performed many miracles and lived a sinless life; He never got married and He never had sex. Jesus died on the cross, not Judas.

John the Baptist called Jesus "the Lamb of God who takes away the sin of the world". Jesus willingly died on the cross on the Jewish feast of Passover so that God would see His innocent blood and 'pass over' our sins and not condemn us to the death we deserve. Jesus was the only prophet to predict His death and resurrection and be seen by hundreds of witnesses after He rose from the dead. Many of you have seen Jesus in your dreams, and you know He is God and He loves you.

[Jesus said,] I am the door: by me if any man enter in, he shall be saved, and shall go in and out, and find pasture. The thief comes not, but for to steal, and to kill, and to destroy: I am come that they might have life, and that they might have it more abundantly. I am the good shepherd: the good shepherd gives his life for the sheep. (John 10:9-11)

Jesus will not pressure you to believe in Him as God and accept Him as your Savior; He wants you to freely choose to love and obey Him. But His gracious offer will end soon, and only those who have accepted Him will continue to be with Him for eternity, while the others who rejected Him will be dismissed from His Presence forever. After the fourth vial, those who worship the Beast of Islam refuse to repent of their sins, so if you're considering becoming a Christian, do so before then. Jesus fulfilled hundreds of Old Testament prophecies before He was born; He will fulfill the Bible prophecies regarding His return.

The 'thief' represents Satan, whom Jesus called "the father of lies;" of course he's going to say the Bible has been corrupted. Jesus said. "*If I do not the works of my Father, believe me not. But if I do, though you believe not me, believe the works: that you may know, and believe, that the Father is in me, and I in him*" (John 10:37-38).

I hope you ask Jesus to save you and give you eternal life.

To All Readers:

Human interpretation of Scripture is faulty, but God's Word remains true, and He will fulfill it. A period of great tribulation is coming in which the seals, trumpets and vials will occur as written in Revelation before the "*great and terrible day of the Lord*".

For then shall be great tribulation, such as was not since the beginning of the world to this time, no, nor ever shall be. And except those days should be shortened, there should no flesh be saved: but for the elect's sake those days shall be shortened. Then if any man shall say to you, See, here is Christ, or there; believe it not. For there shall arise false Christs, and false prophets, and shall show great signs and wonders; so that, if it were possible, they shall deceive the very elect. Behold, I have told you before. Why if they shall say to you, Behold, he is in the desert; go not forth: behold, he is in the secret chambers; believe it not. For as the lightning comes out of the east, and shines even to the west; so shall also the coming of the Son of man be. (Matthew 24:21-27)

Jesus will return from heaven with the clouds in the same manner in which He ascended (Acts 1:9-11), and there will be much lightning and signs in the sky (black sun, red moon, fallen stars) making His return obvious to the whole world. DON'T BELIEVE ANYONE ON EARTH CLAIMING TO BE JESUS CHRIST, THE MESSIAH, regardless of what amazing and miraculous signs he might perform.

Many more Christians will be martyred for their faith. A religious economical system will be imposed upon the world, preventing people from buying or selling unless they receive the mark of allegiance to that religious system. DON'T TAKE THE MARK OF THE BEAST! It would be better to starve to death or be beheaded than to endure the plagues of those who worship the Beast and be thrown into lake of fire with them.

There shall come in the last days scoffers, walking after their own lusts, And saying, Where is the promise of his coming? (2 Peter 5:3b-4b)

DO KEEP BELIEVING IN JESUS' PROMISE TO RETURN.

God's Team and Satan's Team

It is becoming obvious that the religious system Satan will use during the Great Tribulation to destroy Christians and Jews will be Islam. The religious heart of that system is Mecca with its economic port city of Jeddah. "Babylon" is used to refer to the entire religious system of Islam as well as to the city at its heart (Mecca). The Muslim version of a savior is called al-Mahdi, whom Christians would call the Antichrist. Beasts are empires in prophetic scriptures. The Beast of the Earth is referred to as "the false prophet"; and the Beast of the Sea (which appears in Daniel 7 as the 4th beast) is sometimes referred to as the political/religious system, and sometimes referred to as the Antichrist leader who comes from it. The two main religious empires of Islam are Sunni (7-headed beast of sea) and Shia (2-horned beast of earth). The most powerful sect of Sunnism is Wahhabism, which is the whore that rides the 7-headed beast. Just because there are parallels does not mean there is equality of power.

God's Team	Satan's Team
Jerusalem	Babylon (Mecca & Jeddah)
Jesus Christ	Antichrist (Mahdi)
7 Churches	7-headed Beast of Sea (Sunni)
Two Witnesses	2-horned Beast of Earth (Shia)
Bride of Christ	Whore (Wahhabi)
Michael	Destroying Angel from Abyss
other angels	other demons

Book of Revelation

Apocalypse means "lifting of the veil" or "revealing"; hence 'revelation'. The revelation is of Jesus Christ and His Bride; it is a positive word which has only been associated with the tribulations which surround it. The book of the time of the end which Daniel, the beloved prophet, was told to seal (Daniel 12:4) was revealed to John, the beloved apostle, on the isle of Patmos. John used much of Daniel's imagery, and scriptures from many Old Testament prophets.

The Hebrew calendar John used was based upon a 360-day year. The Hebrews had a combined lunar-solar calendar which included a 13th month every six years until reaching the 36th year when an extra month was added to the 40th year. Every forty years this ancient Hebrew 360-day calendar was in sync with the modern 365.25-day calendar.

John was describing things in an orderly fashion, but some things are coupled to others, and some things overlap or coincide with others. If John had hyper-linked text, he could have written a linear time-line of what was to take place. John used the writing style of the Bible in which an outline or overview is given, followed by details, which eventually come back around to the time-line. With this Hebrew cyclical writing style in mind, the prophecies can be grouped according to their timings and commonalities. The seals, trumpets and vials are found in the following chapters of Revelation:

Revelation Chapters

5	Lamb is worthy to break seals
6	Six seals
8	7th seal & 4 trumpets
9	5th & 6th trumpets
11	7th trumpet
14-16	7 vials of wrath

The 7 seals are global in their impact, with the first four seals before the Great Tribulation and the three remaining seals at the end. The 7 vials are poured out on Babylon (Islam) and those who worship the beast, while the 7 trumpets are experienced by the rest of the world; God making a distinction like He did between the Egyptians and the Hebrews. The trumpets and vials are done in tandem [*Encyclopedia of Biblical Prophecy* by J. Barton Payne, p.598, 1973]. The 6th and 7th seal, the 7th vial, and the 7th trumpet are simultaneous, culminating in King Jesus' return to reign and lead His army to victory (Revelation 19).

The Scroll with the Seven Seals: The Marriage Contract

In the Middle East, marriage contracts are still sometimes arranged by parents when their children are very young. Parents were obligated to raise chaste, industrious children who would make good mates.

The scroll in Revelation 5 is the ketubah, or marriage covenant, which has been agreed to and sealed by seven churches (Rev. 2-3) over time, of which we are the last (Laodicea, Rev. 3:14-22). That is why the scroll has 7 seals on it. It was also a Roman custom during Christ's life to have a will witnessed and sealed by seven people. Since Christ's bride-price was His own life, the ketubah scroll is also His will.

I am indebted to Edward Chumney who wrote of the Hebrew marriage traditions and their Biblical fulfillments in "*The Seven Festivals of the Messiah,*" published by Treasure House in 1994.

Hebrew Marriage Traditions	Fulfillment in Scripture
A father chose a bride for his son.	God chose us. Ephesians 1:4
Wedding covenant: witnessed and sealed contract called a *ketubah*.	New covenant is sealed in blood. Jeremiah 31:31; Hebrews 12:24
If the woman drank the wine offered, that <u>sealed the covenant:</u> 'betrothed'.	Disciples drank "new testament" in Christ's blood. (Luke 22:20)
The groom would pay "bride price" to the father of the bride.	Jesus paid Father God with His life-blood, so ketubah is also a will.
Bride accepts a gift from groom; called *kiddushin*, sanctification.	Jesus gave us Holy Spirit, sanctifying and sealing us. Ephesians 1:13; 4:30
Bride had a ritual immersion, and transferred obedience to her husband.	Water baptism and obedience Romans 6-8
Groom returned to his father's house to build an addition: bridal chamber.	New Jerusalem John 14:2-3 and Rev. 21:9-27
Father gave permission to get bride after son constructed bridal chamber.	Until then, only father knew the day and hour of wedding. Mark 13:32-37
Groom to bride's house with shofars, shouting, "the bridegroom comes".	Trumpets are *shofars* (1 Thess. 4:16-17). Matthew 25:6
Wedding ceremony took place under a *chupah*, a white canopy.	Bride meets Groom in clouds. Acts 1:9-11; 1 Thess. 4:14-18
The cantor greeted groom like a king, "Blessed is he who comes".	When Jews chant same, Jesus will come. Matthew 23:39
Vows consummated that night; celebrate wedding feast for 7 days.	John 17 7 days of Tishri 2-9

The opportunity to be included in the new covenant of receiving God's grace through faith in the blood of Jesus Christ becomes successively more difficult with the breaking of each seal, and comes to an end when Jesus breaks the seventh seal. Then those bridal virgins who were prepared will go into the wedding, and those who went back into the world "to buy oil" because they didn't have a personal relationship with Jesus will be shut out (Matthew 25:1-13).

Jesus Purchased the Right to Open the Seven Seals

*In the dispensation of the fulness of times, <u>to re-establish all things in Christ, that are in heaven and on earth,</u> in him. In whom we also are called by lot, being predestinated according to the purpose of him who worketh all things according to the counsel of his will. That we may be unto the praise of his glory: we who before hoped in Christ: In whom you also, after you had heard the word of truth (the gospel of your salvation), in whom also believing, you were signed with the holy Spirit of promise. Who is the pledge of our inheritance, <u>unto the **redemption** of acquisition</u>, unto the praise of his glory. . . .according to the operation of the might of his power, Which he wrought in Christ, raising him up from the dead and setting him on his right hand in the heavenly places. Above all principality and power and virtue and dominion and every name that is named, <u>not only in this world, but also in that which is to come</u>. (Ephesians 1:3-14 edited)*

*For we know that the whole creation groans and travails in pain together until now. And not only they, but ourselves also, which have the first fruits of the Spirit, even we ourselves groan within ourselves, waiting for the adoption, to wit, the **redemption** of our body. (Romans 8:22-23)*

"*Redemption*" in both passages is *apolutrosis*, meaning liberation procured by the payment of a ransom. "*Acquisition*" is *peripoiesis*, meaning possession of one's own property. Jesus gave His life to redeem His own property He created. Jesus prevailed over sin and death. He was the victor in His life, death and resurrection. He was slain to redeem mankind (those written in the Book of Life) and the earth. Jesus will remove the curse and all its effects from the earth, and God will make a new heaven and earth (2 Peter 3:13). Believers await our new resurrection bodies which we acquire when we die or when Christ returns and raptures those of us who are still alive. And then we shall reign with Christ on the new earth He creates.

And I saw in the right hand of him that sat on the throne a book written within and on the backside, sealed with seven seals. . . . And I wept much, because no man was found worthy to open and to read the book, neither to look thereon. And one of the elders said to me, Weep not: behold, the Lion of the tribe of

*Juda, the Root of David, has prevailed to open the book, and to loose the seven seals thereof. . . . And he came and took the book out of the right hand of him that sat on the throne. And when he had taken the book, the four beasts and four and twenty elders fell down before the Lamb, having every one of them harps, and <u>golden vials full of odors, which are the prayers of saints</u>. And they sung a new song, saying, You are worthy to take the book, and to open the seals thereof: for you were slain, and have **redeemed** us to God by your blood out of every kindred, and tongue, and people, and nation; And have made us to our God kings and priests: and we shall reign on the earth. And I beheld, and I heard the voice of many angels round about the throne and the beasts and the elders: and the number of them was ten thousand times ten thousand, and thousands of thousands; Saying with a loud voice, Worthy is the Lamb that was slain to receive power, and riches, and wisdom, and strength, and honor, and glory, and blessing. (Revelation 5:1-12 edited)*

"*Redeemed*" is *agorazo*, meaning purchased. After all the seals have been opened, Jesus will receive His purchased possession, His Bride; and He will receive all power and authority as King over the whole earth, and His saints will serve Him and bless Him and give King Jesus the riches and honor He deserves.

When God delivered the Hebrews from Egypt and plagued the Egyptians and destroyed the Egyptian army, it was in answer to prayers (Exodus 3:7-10). Similarly, Christians have been crying out to God for deliverance from Muslim oppression. The cries of millions of faithful martyrs has been heard and stored as fragrant aromas in 24 golden vials. In Revelation 15:7, "*one of the four beasts gave to the seven angels seven golden vials full of the wrath of God.*" Whether these seven are from the twenty-four is not stated; nor does it say golden vials full of prayers have now become vials full of God's wrath. But these prayers may have been imprecations seeking God's destruction of their enemies like in Psalm 83, or seeking temporary hardship of their enemy to bring repentance (Acts 13:8-12).

The 7th angel will cast this golden censer to the earth when the 7th seal is broken. There is a special golden censer used in the Holy of Holies (Hebrews 9:3-4) which is patterned on the one used in heaven. It too is associated with God's wrath and the prayers of the saints.

Though there are seven each of the seals, trumpets and vials; the first group of four of each object is a distinct grouping. The first four trumpets and vials parallel each other as they make a distinction between those who worship the Beast of Islam, and those who do not. Prior to them and the beginning of the Great Tribulation are the first four seals.

Four Horsemen (Seals #1-4)

There have always been conquerors bent on taking over the world, and wars, and economic problems and death in various places of the globe; but the four horsemen are felt by the whole world at the same time. They are a prelude to the 3 ½ year Great Tribulation to awaken the world out of its slumber, yet they will continue into the Great Tribulation. September 11th is the day Jesus was born in 3 B.C.; it was Rosh HaShanah, Jewish New Year. Using September 11th and dates near Rosh HaShanah was a way to awaken Christ's Bride as to His soon return.

Seal #1

*And I saw when the Lamb opened one of the seals, and I heard, as it were the noise of thunder, one of the four beasts saying, Come and see. And I saw, and behold a **white horse**: and he that sat on him had a bow; and a crown was given to him: and he went forth conquering, and to conquer. (Revelation 6:1-2)*

The four horsemen have already begun. They precede the 3 1/2 year Great Tribulation, and are a wake-up call to the world that something big is about to happen. Though Islamic terrorists had bombed many embassies worldwide, it was the attack on September 11, 2001 (Rosh HaShanah was a week later) which awakened the world to the "peaceful" white horse of Islam attempting to conquer the world without "*arrows*" (nukes). To view Islam's violent toll of conquest, visit www.thereligionofpeace.com which keeps track of each attack worldwide.

New York City

And I will give power to my <u>two witnesses</u>, and they shall prophesy a thousand two hundred and three score days, clothed in sackcloth. These are the <u>two olive trees</u>, and the <u>two candlesticks</u> standing before the God of the earth. . . .And their *dead bodies shall lie in the street of the great city, which spiritually is called Sodom and Egypt, where also our Lord was crucified. And they of the people and kindreds and tongues and nations shall see their dead bodies three days and an half, and shall not suffer their dead bodies to be put in graves. And they that dwell on the earth shall rejoice over them, and make merry, and shall send gifts one to another; because these two prophets tormented them that dwelled on the earth. And after three days and an half the spirit of life from God entered into them, and they stood on their feet; and great fear fell on them which saw them. And they heard a great voice from heaven saying to them, Come up here. And they ascended up to heaven in a cloud; and their enemies beheld them. (Revelation 11:8-12)*

During the Revolutionary War New York City was greatly damaged twice by fires, laid siege to, and had many battles fought there with patriots crying, "No king but King Jesus!" From 1788 to 1790, New York City was the capital of the United States of America. (Jerusalem is Israel's capital in which Jesus was crucified as King of the Jews, and later laid siege to and burned.) New York City is the most populous city ("*great city*") of the United States with over eight million people, and it is the city with the largest Jewish population outside of Israel (like Egypt housed the Hebrews for hundreds of years). It also has a large homosexual community ("*Sodom*").

On **September 11**, 2001 Islamic terrorists flew planes into the Twin Towers, and about 3,000 people from 90 different countries died. The Muslims in Palestine were shown dancing in the streets and celebrating by passing out candy. This was the "white horse" of the first seal, and something similar may occur on April 6, 2009. Muslims have been slaughtering Christians around the world and leaving their corpses to rot. The "*three and a half days*" refers to the years of the Great Tribulation in which there will be more martyrs. The slaughter of believers will continue and increase until September 16, 2012 when the heavens and earth will shake at the Lord's coming, and He will call His people to Him.

The two witnesses, olive trees and candlesticks represent God's two anointed 'sons' (Zechariah 4:14); the believing Jews and Gentiles. "*Witness*" is *marturos*, another word for 'martyr'. Those who died in the 9/11 attacks were martyred for living in a Christian country which protected the Jews. The Twin Towers are not the "*two witnesses*", but are a symbol of martyrdom.

The mastermind of the 9/11 attack, and many other Al Qaeda attacks, was Khalid Sheikh Mohammed who was born in Pakistan but received his mechanical engineering degree in the US. According to notes of his interrogation on the internet titled "Substitution for the Testimony of Khalid Sheikh Mohammed," "Sheikh Mohammed said that the purpose of the attack on the Twin Towers was to 'wake the American people up'."

*I will also gather all nations, and will bring them down into the valley of Jehoshaphat, and will plead with them there for my people and for my heritage Israel, whom they have scattered among the nations, and parted my land. Proclaim you this among the Gentiles; Prepare war, **wake up** the mighty men, let all the men of war draw near; let them come up: Let the heathen be wakened, and come up to the valley of Jehoshaphat: for there will I sit to judge all the heathen round about. (Joel 3:2, 9, 12)*

The purpose of the first four seals is to get people to "*wake up*" and recognize God's judgment is coming soon. That judgment includes how we have treated the Jews and the land which God gave them.

"On **September 11**, 2008 US Consul General Jacob Walles admitted during an interview with a Palestinian newspaper that there were secret negotiations taking place to divide Jerusalem. The US State Department and Israeli officials were quick to deny such negotiation. Consul General Walles is second in command under the US ambassador to Israel and knows what is going on. I feel he let "the cat out of the bag." Walles' statement was in perfect agreement with Secretary Rice's actions. This admission by the Consul General was on Thursday, September 11. At the very time of this admission, Hurricane Ike was rushing toward Texas. This was a massive hurricane 600 miles wide! It struck late Friday and the eye went directly up Galveston Bay. Entire towns were destroyed and Houston was crippled. The rippling effect is not known at this time. The damaged is estimated now at $20 billion and counting. This was bad enough but then Lehman Brothers, one of the largest Wall Street banks, collapsed right on the heels of the hurricane. Then the domino effect hit the stock market." [John McTernan from http://johnmcternansinsights.blogspot.com, emphasis added]

Seal #2

*And when he had opened the second seal, I heard the second beast say, Come and see. And there went out another **horse** that was **red**: and power was given to him that sat thereon to take peace from the earth, and that they should kill one another: and there was given to him a great sword. (Revelation 6:3-4)*

The red horse of Islamic terrorism has "*taken peace from the earth*". Not content to just kill infidels, the Muslims also kill other Muslims ("*they should kill one another*"). On **September 11**, 2006 a 12-year-old boy was among six people murdered by a suicide bomber at a funeral for a previous victim of a suicide bombing in Afghanistan; thirty-six were wounded.

Seal #3

*And when he had opened the third seal, I heard the third beast say, Come and see. And I beheld, and see a **black horse**; and he that sat on him had a pair of balances in his hand. And I heard a voice in the middle of the four beasts say, A measure of wheat for a penny, and three measures of barley for a penny; and see you hurt not the oil and the wine. (Revelation 6:5-6)*

Again it was during the "days of awe" between Rosh Hashanah and Yom Kippur (Sept. 29 and Oct. 9, 2008) that the black horse of economic ruin traveled the globe. (Was it just Democrats causing runs on banks to create economic uncertainty to shift the focus off of the war in Iraq so that their candidate would be elected? Or were rich terrorists making large computer transactions ½ hour before closing for twelve days?) One day's worth of food for one day's wage is mere subsistence. There may yet come a blight on wheat and barley until it gets to the point where "daily bread" will cost a day's wages (Rev. 6:6).

Seal #4

*And when he had opened the fourth seal, I heard the voice of the fourth beast say, Come and see. And I looked, and behold a **pale horse**: and his name that sat on him was Death, and Hell followed with him. And power was given to them over the fourth part of the earth, to kill with sword, and with hunger, and with death, and with the beasts of the earth. (Revelation 6:7-8)*

Then comes the pale horse of Death. Currently Islam has a majority in one fourth of the world. Russia still has a large Muslim population even after all the "-istan" secessions. Current Muslim world population is estimated between 21% and 27%. And in those parts of the world in which Islam has power, it is killing through war and famine. All this chaos before the 3 1/2 year clock of the Great Tribulation even begins, but they will continue through it.

What Event Started the 3 1/2 Year Clock?

God started the Great Tribulation clock. God told Michael to release Satan, and Satan *"knows that his time is short"*. Counting backwards 1,260 days from September 16, 2012, the Great Tribulation clock began on April 6, 2009. On that day a unique sign in the heavens was reported by Fox News: "In a new image from NASA's Chandra X-ray Observatory, high-energy X-rays emanating from the nebula around PSR B1509-58 have been colored blue to reveal a structure resembling a hand reaching for some eternal red cosmic light."

> *Your hand shall find out all your enemies: <u>your right hand shall find out those that hate you. You shall make them as a fiery oven in the time of your anger</u>: the LORD shall swallow them up in his wrath, and the fire shall devour them. Their fruit shall you destroy from the earth, and their seed from among the children of men. **For they intended evil against you: they imagined a mischievous device, which they are not able to perform**. Therefore shall you make them turn their back, when you shall make ready your arrows on your strings against the face of them. (Psalms 21:8-12)*

I pray that the terrorists are unable to secure or produce a nuclear weapon ("*mischievous device*") before Christ returns.

Power and Influence of USA Is Removed

For God to accomplish what He intends to do in the Middle East, He needed to remove the United States of America (2 Thess. 2:3-8). The black horse of economic ruin has already removed the US dollar as the standard of world currency, and continued reckless government spending will keep it suppressed.

On April 6, 2009, President Obama declared to the Turkey parliament, "Let me say this as clearly as I can: The United States is not, and will never be, at war with Islam." He further clarified, "Our partnership with the Muslim world is critical in rolling back a fringe ideology that people of all faiths reject." President Obama continued, "But I also want to be clear that America's relationship with the Muslim world cannot and will not be based on opposition to al Qaeda. Far from it. We seek broad engagement based upon mutual interests and mutual respect. We will listen carefully, bridge misunderstanding, and seek common ground." Each demonstration of American weakness and withdrawal emboldens the jihadists. Now with America subdued, the Antichrist may soon appear and declare himself to be god.

There are three three woes which are time markers. The first woe begins five months of locusts. The second woe begins the Armegeddon War which lasts for one year, one month, one day, and one hour. The third woe is the 7th trumpet which begins the Day of the Lord. There are also three angelic announcements at the beginning of the Great Tribulation. The first angelic announcement is the everlasting gospel with a loud voice to the world (Rev. 14:6-7).

Babylon is Fallen

The second angelic announcement is the fall of the great city Babylon (Mecca), taken out by a meteor or a bomb. According to "The Samson Option" written by reporter Seymour Hersh, Israel may have 200 to 400 atomic warheads, ready to use as a last resort to preserve the existence of the country. Osama bin Laden has denounced the house of Saud and let it be known that he is ready to attack oil cities in his home nation of Saudi Arabia in order to crush the economy of the rest of the world. Osama is a Sunni, but most of Saudi Arabia is Wahhabi (apostates according to Sunnis). Al-Qaeda might bomb Mecca and its port city Jeddah. "*Osama*" is lion in Arabic.

The burden of the desert of the sea. As whirlwinds in the south pass through; so it comes from the desert, from a terrible land. A grievous vision is declared to me; the treacherous dealer deals treacherously, and the spoiler spoils. Go up, O Elam: besiege, O Media; all the sighing thereof have I made to cease. Therefore are my loins filled with pain: pangs have taken hold on me, as the pangs of a woman that travails: I was bowed down at the hearing of it; I was dismayed at the seeing of it. . . . And he cried, A lion: My lord, I stand continually on the watchtower in the daytime, and I am set in my ward whole nights: And, behold, here comes a chariot of men, with a couple of horsemen. And he answered and said, Babylon is fallen, is fallen; and all

*the graven images of her gods he has broken to the ground. . . .
The burden of Dumah. . . . The burden on Arabia. In the forest
in Arabia shall you lodge, O you traveling companies of
Dedanim. . . .The inhabitants of the land of Tema brought water
to him that was thirsty, they prevented with their bread him that
fled. For they fled from the swords, from the drawn sword, and
from the bent bow, and from the grievousness of war. For thus
has the LORD said to me, Within a year, according to the years
of an hireling, and all the glory of Kedar shall fail: And the
residue of the number of archers, the mighty men of the children
of Kedar, shall be diminished: for the LORD God of Israel has
spoken it. (Isaiah 21:1-17 edited)*

The Elamites lived in what is now the province of Khuzestan, Iran which borders the Persian Gulf. The name "Persia" was not used until after Babylonian captivity. And Media is the Medes (now Afghanistan). Though Persia has borders with seas, its desert is inland. The Medes and Persians did besiege and conquer Babylon more than a hundred years after this prophecy.

This burden or oracle also has a future fulfillment regarding Arabia. Dumah is now called Dumat el Janda, located near Medina. Dumah and Kedar were sons of Ishmael, Abraham's son by Hagar. Mohammed was of the lineage of Kedar. Mohammed first promoted his new religion in Mecca, who cast him out. He fled north to Medina. Continuing on the road north of Medina are Hafirat al Ayda (where Dedan settled) and Tayma (Tema). Medina accepted his religion and authority, and Mohammed returned to Mecca with armed men from Medina. Mohammed threw out all the idols from Mecca, except the Kaaba to the moon god which he then proclaimed to be "The Deity" (Al-Ilah, which was shortened to Allah). The Hebrew words for "*fail*" and "*diminished*" could also be translated to bring Kedar to an 'end' and to 'bring to nothing'. Arabian desert of the sea is prophetically connected to Babylon and the Medes and Persians destruction of it, and it will fall within a 360-day year of the announcement of its destruction.

With the Wahhabis and Saudi oil out of the way, the Beast of the Earth (the Shia of Afghanistan and Iran), will then require all people to wear a mark of allegiance to Islam on their arm or forehead in order to buy or sell, and eventually to be killed if they refuse the mark. The third angelic announcement is if anyone worships the Beast or takes its mark, he will also experience God's wrath poured out on the Beast.

First Four Trumpets and Vials

The first angel sounded, and there followed hail and fire mingled with blood, and they were cast on the earth: and the third part of trees was burnt up, and all green grass was burnt up. And the second angel sounded, and as it were <u>a great mountain burning</u> with fire was cast into the sea: and the third part of the sea became blood; And the third part of the creatures which were in the sea, and had life, died; and the third part of the ships were destroyed. And the third angel sounded, and there fell <u>a great star from heaven, burning</u> as it were a lamp, and it fell on the third part of the rivers, and on the fountains of waters; And the name of the star is called Wormwood: and the third part of the waters became wormwood; and many men died of the waters, because they were made bitter. And the fourth angel sounded, and the third part of the sun was smitten, and the third part of the moon, and the third part of the stars; so as the third part of them was darkened, and the day shone not for a third part of it, and the night likewise. (Revelation 8:7-12)

At the first trumpet "hail and fire mingled with blood" (Rev. 8:7) were cast on the earth. It may be literal blood, or it may be a clue that biological weapons will be used. Blood is weaponized throughout the first four trumpets and vials. The second trumpet has something like a great burning mountain which is thrown into the sea, whereas the third trumpet states a great burning star fell from heaven; one sounds man-made while the other sounds God-made. The fourth trumpet takes away one third of daylight and night light, but it does not make a black sun and a red moon as the 6th seal does.

It is unclear when in the first two years of the Great Tribulation these sets of four will occur, or how much time is allotted to each or between each. The Sea of Babylon is most likely the Arabian Sea surrounding the Arabian Peninsula with its arms of the Red Sea, Gulf of Oman, and the Persian Gulf.

First Four Trumpets (upon world)
1st All grass burnt; 1/3 trees
2nd 1/3 sea, sea-life & ships
3rd 1/3 rivers; & bitter waters
4th 1/3 of sun, moon & stars

First Four Vials (upon Babylon)
1st Sores upon worshipers of Beast
2nd Sea to blood; all sea-life dies
3rd All rivers and fountains to blood
4th Use sun to scorch men with fire

And I heard the angel of the waters say, You are righteous, O Lord, which are, and were, and shall be, because you have judged thus. For they have shed the blood of saints and prophets, and you have given them blood to drink; for they are worthy. And I heard another out of the altar say, Even so, Lord God Almighty, true and righteous are your judgments. And the fourth angel poured out his vial on the sun; and power was given to him to scorch men with fire. And men were scorched with great heat, and blasphemed the name of God, which has power over these plagues: and they repented not to give him glory. (Revelation 16:5-9)

There is no statement that the people of "Babylon" repent from this time forward. Their murderous acts have made them are "worthy" of the judgment of a righteous God. Even though the sun has already had one third of its light removed, it still has the ability to scorch with great heat. The sun's last cycle of sun spots went unusually long, and it may result in solar flares.

5th Trumpet and Vial (First Woe)

And there came out of the smoke locusts on the earth: and to them was given power, as the scorpions of the earth have power. And it was commanded them that they should not hurt the grass of the earth, neither any green thing, neither any tree; but only those men which have not the seal of God in their foreheads. And to them it was given that they should not kill them, but that they should be tormented five months: and their torment was as the torment of a scorpion, when he strikes a man. And in those days shall men seek death, and shall not find it; and shall desire to die, and death shall flee from them. And the shapes of the locusts were like to horses prepared to battle; and on their heads were as it were crowns like gold, and their faces were as the faces of men. And they had hair as the hair of women, and their teeth were as the teeth of lions. And they had breastplates, as it were breastplates of iron; and the sound of their wings was as the sound of chariots of many horses running to battle. And they had tails like to scorpions, and there were stings in their tails: and their power was to hurt men five months.(Rev. 9:3-10)

John, the apostle, is trying to describe something he's never seen before by relating it to things he knows. Locusts with breastplates of iron with the roar of their wings like many chariots, yet with men's faces best describes helicopters. The women's hair may be rope ladders. The sting could be biological or chemical weapons spewed from their "tails", or traditional weapons. Counting backwards from the date of Christ's return as September 16, 2012, the fifth trumpet and fifth vial should commence on March 26, 2011.

And the fifth angel poured out his vial on the seat of the beast; and his kingdom was full of darkness; and they gnawed their tongues for pain, And blasphemed the God of heaven because of their pains and their sores, and repented not of their deeds. (Revelation 16:10-11)

"Darkness" is *skotoo,* meaning to obscure or blind. This word is only used once in the New Testament; usually *skotos* or *skotinos* are used for outer or inner darkness respectively. It may be that the chemical warfare produces very painful sores and cloudy vision. The pattern after the fourth and fifth vials is that the Beast worshipers cursed the God of heaven and did not repent.

5th Seal (Great Tribulation Martyrs)

And when he had opened the fifth seal, I saw under the altar the souls of them that were slain for the word of God, and for the testimony which they held: And they cried with a loud voice, saying, How long, O Lord, holy and true, do you not judge and avenge our blood on them that dwell on the earth? And white robes were given to every one of them; and it was said to them, that they should rest yet for a little season, until their fellow servants also and their brothers, that should be killed as they were, should be fulfilled. (Revelation 6:9-11)

After this I beheld, and, see, a great multitude, which no man could number, of all nations, and kindreds, and people, and tongues, stood before the throne, and before the Lamb, clothed with white robes, and palms in their hands; And cried with a loud voice, saying, Salvation to our God which sits on the throne, and to the Lamb. . . . And one of the elders answered, saying to me, What are these which are arrayed in white robes? and from where came they? And I said to him, Sir, you know.

And he said to me, These are they which came out of great tribulation, and have washed their robes, and made them white in the blood of the Lamb. Therefore are they before the throne of God, and serve him day and night in his temple: and he that sits on the throne shall dwell among them. They shall hunger no more, neither thirst any more; neither shall the sun light on them, nor any heat. For the Lamb which is in the middle of the throne shall feed them, and shall lead them to living fountains of waters: and God shall wipe away all tears from their eyes. (Revelation 7:9-17 edited)

These courageous saints will be persecuted for their faith. They will be hungry and thirsty, possibly because they refuse the mark of the Beast and can not buy or sell. They will be killed for following Jesus, but then their King will feed and comfort them. Since they only wait a *"little season"*, this seal occurs during the Armegeddon War before Jesus' return.

6th Vial and Trumpet (Armageddon War: Second Woe)

With the 6th trumpet and vial the prior distinction between them (vials upon Babylon and trumpets upon the rest of the world) is blurred as they all are brought together to Mount Megiddo in Israel. The word for mountain is *Har*, and so we get (H)ar Megiddo(n), or Armegeddon. The 6th vial dries up the Euphrates so the kings of the east can more easily transport their armies to Israel. Whether this is accomplished using a man-made dam, weather conditions, or a miracle is unclear. Three demons are sent to entice kings to make war at Armegeddon.

Countries immediately east of the Euphrates river are Shiite south-eastern Iraq, Shiite Iran and Afghanistan which constitute the Shia Beast of the Earth. These countries are what used to be the Persian empire. The Persian empire once sought to exterminate the Jews, when Queen Esther foiled their plans (Purim); but they are planning to do so again, and this time with nuclear weapons.

*And the sixth angel poured out his vial on the great river **Euphrates**; and the water thereof was dried up, that the way of the kings of the east might be prepared. And I saw three unclean spirits like frogs come out of the mouth of the dragon, and out of the mouth of the beast, and out of the mouth of the false prophet. For they are the spirits of devils, working miracles, which go forth to the kings of the earth and of the whole world, to gather them to the battle of that great day of God Almighty.*

Behold, I come as a thief. Blessed is he that watches, and keeps his garments, lest he walk naked, and they see his shame. And he gathered them together into a place called in the Hebrew tongue Armageddon. (Revelation 16:12-16)

*And the sixth angel sounded, and I heard a voice from the four horns of the golden altar which is before God, Saying to the sixth angel which had the trumpet, Loose the four angels which are bound in the great river **Euphrates**. And the four angels were loosed, which were prepared for an hour, and a day, and a month, and a year, for to slay the third part of men. And the number of the army of the horsemen were two hundred thousand thousand: and I heard the number of them. And thus I saw the horses in the vision, and them that sat on them, having breastplates of fire, and of jacinth, and brimstone: and the heads of the horses were as the heads of lions; and out of their mouths issued fire and smoke and brimstone. By these three was the third part of men killed, by the fire, and by the smoke, and by the brimstone, which issued out of their mouths. For their power is in their mouth, and in their tails: for their tails were like to serpents, and had heads, and with them they do hurt. And the rest of the men which were not killed by these plagues yet repented not of the works of their hands, that they should not worship devils, and idols of gold, and silver, and brass, and stone, and of wood: which neither can see, nor hear, nor walk: Neither repented they of their murders, nor of their sorceries, nor of their fornication, nor of their thefts. (Revelation 8:13-21)*

This time John seems to be describing fire-throwing tanks with small caliber weapons in their rear, along with a two hundred million man army. The people are killed by the fire, smoke, and brimstone which are then called plagues; so this is chemical warfare. This time it is recorded under the trumpet that the survivors of the world who worshiped other gods did not repent.

The breastplates are fire, jacinth, and brimstone. Jacinth (hyacinth) flower is blue; the stone is a lustrous orange-yellow, orange-red, or yellow-brown; but when it's cut and polished it is blue-white. Brimstone (sulfur) is naturally yellow, red when melted, and burns blue. Red, orange, brown, blue, and yellow may be colors of a new U.N. army or new Muslim army, even though the preferred color representing Islam is green. More likely, John is describing fire protective gear.

Using the 360-day calendar, "*a day, and a month, and a year*" equals 391 days. The year 2012 on our calendar is a leap year having one extra day. Counting backwards 391 days from the calculated date of Christ's return on September 16, 2012, the war of Armegeddon should commence on August 23, 2011.

Mount (*Har*) Meggido overlooks the Valley of Esdraelon. Mount Gilboa to its east overlooks the Valley of Jezreel. The armies will be gathered to these valleys, scripturally known as the "valley of Jehosphat (God's judgment)" and "the valley of decision", where God plans to destroy them.

6th Seal: Jerusalem Will Be Divided Into Three Parts

And the great city was divided into three parts, and the cities of the nations fell: and great Babylon came in remembrance before God, to give to her the cup of the wine of the fierceness of his wrath. And every island fled away, and the mountains were not found. (Revelation 16:19-20)

"Great city" refers to both Jerusalem and Babylon; but here, Jerusalem is mentioned first. One of the divisions will be the Mount of Olives (Zechariah 14:4) to make a way of escape for Jews out of the city. The description of islands and mountains vanishing may be the result of soil liquefaction in which soil suddenly goes from a solid state to a liquefied state, like quicksand. This occurred in the 1964 earthquakes in Japan and Alaska.

And I beheld when he had opened the sixth seal, and, see, there was a great earthquake; and the sun became black as sackcloth of hair, and the moon became as blood; And the stars of heaven fell to the earth, even as a fig tree casts her untimely figs, when she is shaken of a mighty wind. And the heaven departed as a scroll when it is rolled together; and every mountain and island were moved out of their places. And the kings of the earth, and the great men, and the rich men, and the chief captains, and the mighty men, and every slave, and every free man, hid themselves in the dens and in the rocks of the mountains; And said to the mountains and rocks, Fall on us, and hide us from the face of him that sits on the throne, and from the wrath of the Lamb: For the great day of his wrath is come; and who shall be able to stand? (Revelation 6:12-17)

Enter into the rock, and hide you in the dust, for fear of the LORD, and for the glory of his majesty. The lofty looks of man shall be humbled, and the haughtiness of men shall be bowed down, and the LORD alone shall be exalted in that day. For the day of the LORD of hosts shall be on every one that is proud and lofty, and on every one that is lifted up; and he shall be brought low: . . . And the loftiness of man shall be bowed down, and the haughtiness of men shall be made low: and the LORD alone shall be exalted in that day. And the idols he shall utterly abolish. And they shall go into the holes of the rocks, and into the caves of the earth, for fear of the LORD, and for the glory of his majesty, when he rises to shake terribly the earth. In that day a man shall cast his idols of silver, and his idols of gold, which they made each one for himself to worship, to the moles and to the bats; To go into the clefts of the rocks, and into the tops of the ragged rocks, for fear of the LORD, and for the glory of his majesty, when he rises to shake terribly the earth. (Isaiah 2:10-21 edited)

Just like Adam and Eve, sinners will seek in vain to hide from the LORD. The severity of the global "earth shake" just prior to Christ's return is unimaginable. No one will be able to stand physically but will all be brought to their hands and knees or faces, and they will have to acknowledge the Creator of Heaven and Earth and humble themselves before the majesty of His appearing.

Dark Sun and Moon

The heavens and earth are falling apart, and people cry out for a quick death and to be hidden from the coming Judge and judgment. God will humble the wicked. The sun and moon have been at two-thirds strength, and now they're getting dimmer. A dark sun and moon were common prophetic signs of Our Lord's imminent return as Judge Jesus.

Behold, the day of the LORD comes, cruel both with wrath and fierce anger, to lay the land desolate: and he shall destroy the sinners thereof out of it. For the stars of heaven and the constellations thereof shall not give their light: the sun shall be darkened in his going forth, and the moon shall not cause her light to shine. And I will punish the world for their evil, and the wicked for their iniquity; and I will cause the arrogance of the

proud to cease, and will lay low the haughtiness of the terrible.
(Isaiah 13:9-11)

The earth shall quake before them; the heavens shall tremble:
the sun and the moon shall be dark, and the stars shall withdraw
their shining: And the LORD shall utter his voice before his
army: for his camp is very great: for he is strong that executes
his word: for the day of the LORD is great and very terrible;
and who can abide it? Therefore also now, said the LORD, turn
you even to me with all your heart, and with fasting, and with
weeping, and with mourning: And rend your heart, and not your
garments, and turn to the LORD your God: for he is gracious
and merciful, slow to anger, and of great kindness, and repents
him of the evil. . . . And I will show wonders in the heavens and
in the earth, blood, and fire, and pillars of smoke. The sun shall
be turned into darkness, and the moon into blood, before the
great and terrible day of the LORD come. (Joel 2:10-13, 31)

Signs Immediately Before Christ's Second Coming: (Voices, Lightning, Thunder, Hail, and Earthquake)

And out of the throne proceeded lightning and thunder and
voices: and there were seven lamps of fire burning before the
throne, which are the seven Spirits of God. (Revelation 4:5)

I have looked, and behold a candlestick all of gold, with a bowl
on the top of it, and his seven lamps thereon, and seven pipes to
the seven lamps, which are on the top thereof: . . . This is the
word of the LORD to Zerubbabel, saying, Not by might, nor by
power, but by my spirit, said the LORD of hosts. Who are you, O
great mountain? before Zerubbabel you shall become a plain:
and he shall bring forth the headstone thereof with shoutings,
crying, Grace, grace to it. Moreover the word of the LORD
came to me, saying, The hands of Zerubbabel have laid the
foundation of this house; his hands shall also finish it; and you
shall know that the LORD of hosts has sent me to you. For who
has despised the day of small things? for they shall rejoice, and
shall see the plummet in the hand of Zerubbabel with those
seven; they are the eyes of the LORD, which run to and fro
through the whole earth. (Zechariah 4:2-10)

From the throne of God proceed lightning and thunder and voices. On the Day of the LORD everyone will experience a glimpse of God's majesty from His throne in heaven as His kingdom comes to be established upon the earth. Christ's kingdom had "*small beginnings*" upon the earth, but the earth shall be leveled before Him, and He shall build His temple and kingdom on earth with Himself as the "cornerstone". Those of the seven churches of God throughout history will rejoice. The following events are in very quick succession.

7th Vial

And I saw another sign in heaven, great and marvelous, seven angels having the seven last plagues; for in them is filled up the wrath of God. . . . And the temple was filled with smoke from the glory of God, and from his power; and no man was able to enter into the temple, till the seven plagues of the seven angels were fulfilled. (Revelation 15:1, 8)

The seven "*last*" is *eschatos*, meaning end of or final; from which we get the word eschatology. These seven vials of plagues upon Babylon must be fulfilled and concluded prior to the 7th trumpet.

And the seventh angel poured out his vial into the air; and there came a great voice out of the temple of heaven, from the throne, saying, It is done. And there were <u>voices, and thunders, and lightning; and there was a great earthquake,</u> such as was not since men were on the earth, so mighty an earthquake, and so great. And the great city was divided into three parts, and the cities of the nations fell: and great Babylon came in remembrance before God, to give to her the cup of the wine of the fierceness of his wrath. And every island fled away, and the mountains were not found. And there fell on men a <u>great hail</u> out of heaven, every stone about the weight of a talent: and men blasphemed God because of the plague of the hail; for the plague thereof was exceeding great. (Revelation 16:17-21)

7th Seal

And when he had opened the seventh seal, there was silence in heaven about the space of half an hour. . . .And another angel came and stood at the altar, having a golden censer; and there was given to him much incense, that he should offer it with the *prayers of all saints on the golden altar which was before the throne. And the smoke of the incense, which came with the prayers of the saints, ascended up before God out of the angel's hand. And the angel took the censer, and filled it with fire of the altar, and cast it into the earth: and there were <u>voices, and thunder, and lightning, and an earthquake.</u> (Rev. 8:1-5 edited)*

7th Trumpet: Third Woe

*There should be **time no longer**: But in the days of the voice of the seventh angel, when he shall begin to sound, the mystery of God should be **finished**, as he has declared to his servants the prophets. (Revelation 10:6d-7)*

The second woe is past; and, behold, the third woe comes quickly. And the seventh angel sounded; and there were great voices in heaven, saying, The kingdoms of this world are become the kingdoms of our Lord, and of his Christ; and he shall reign for ever and ever. And the four and twenty elders, which sat before God on their seats, fell on their faces, and worshipped God, Saying, We give you thanks, O LORD God Almighty, which are, and were, and are to come; because you have taken to you your great power, and have reigned. And the nations were angry, and your wrath is come, and the time of the dead, that they should be judged, and that you should give reward to your servants the prophets, and to the saints, and them that fear your name, small and great; and should destroy them which destroy the earth. And the temple of God was opened in heaven, and there was seen in his temple the ark of his testament: and there were <u>lightning, and voices, and thunder, and an earthquake, and great hail</u>. (Revelation 11:14-19)

"*Time no longer*" means no further delay. It is the same word (*teleo*) translated "*finished*" here and when Jesus cried "*It is finished*" (John 19:30) from the cross.   God's master plan comes to completion in King Jesus ruling and reigning the nations through the consummation of His wrath and judgment.

King Jesus Returns and Fights, and Reigns

The following passage is directed to Jerusalem, "*the city where David dwelled*" but prophetically calling it "*Ariel*" which means 'lion of

God'. Thus it is a prophecy regarding when Jerusalem shall become the city of the "*Lion of the tribe of Judah*" who was called "*the son of David*", Jesus Christ. King Jesus will defeat all the nations who come against Israel.

*Moreover the multitude of your strangers shall be like small dust, and the multitude of the terrible ones shall be as chaff that passes away: yes, it shall be at an instant suddenly. You shall be visited of the LORD of hosts <u>with thunder, and with earthquake, and great noise, with storm and tempest, and the flame of devouring fire</u>. And the multitude of all the nations that fight against Ariel, even all that fight against her and her fortification, and that distress her, shall be as a dream of a night vision. . . . For the LORD has poured out on you the spirit of deep sleep, and has closed your eyes: <u>the prophets and your rulers, the seers has he covered. And the vision of all is become to you as the words of a book that is sealed</u>, . . . Woe to them that seek deep to hide their counsel from the LORD, and their works are in the dark, and they say, Who sees us? and who knows us? <u>Surely your turning of things upside down shall be esteemed as the potter's clay:</u> for shall the work say of him that made it, He made me not? or shall the thing framed say of him that framed it, He had no understanding? Is it not yet a very little while, and **Lebanon** shall be turned into a fruitful field, and the fruitful field shall be esteemed as a forest? And in that day shall the deaf hear the words of the book, and the eyes of the blind shall see out of obscurity, and out of darkness. The meek also shall increase their joy in the LORD, and the poor among men shall rejoice in the Holy One of Israel. <u>For the terrible one is brought to nothing, and the scorner is consumed, and all that watch for iniquity are cut off:</u> That make a man an offender for a word, and lay a snare for him that reproves in the gate, and turn aside the just for a thing of nothing. Therefore thus said the LORD, who redeemed Abraham, concerning the house of Jacob, Jacob shall not now be ashamed, neither shall his face now wax pale. But when he sees his children, the work of my hands, in the middle of him, they shall sanctify my name, and sanctify the Holy One of Jacob, and shall fear the God of Israel. They also that erred in spirit shall come to understanding, and they that murmured shall learn doctrine. (Isaiah 29:5-24 edited)*

Sadly, the Jewish rulers and prophets will not understand the prophecies regarding the end-times in which they live. They will focus more on the oral traditions of the elders (Matthew 15:1-20), the *Mishnah*, which caused them to be blinded to Christ's first coming. But God, the Potter (Isaiah 64:8), will use His vessels according to His own plans (Romans 9:20-28; Rev. 2:25-27). The restoration of Jewish Israel was also a restoration of Christian Lebanon (until the Shia Muslims took over). Christians began to understand end-times better only after Israel became a nation again, and began to look for the "*terrible one*", the Antichrist, whom God will destroy. A person that "*reproves in the gate*" is a leader of the city. And the Jews shall also come to understand their place in prophecy. Israel's prime minister Netanyahu is going to have people come after him over trivial matters, and those within his government will try to overturn his plans.

> *Behold, the day of the LORD comes, and your spoil shall be divided in the middle of you. For I will gather all nations against Jerusalem to battle; and the city shall be taken, and the houses rifled, and the women ravished; and half of the city shall go forth into captivity, and the residue of the people shall not be cut off from the city. Then shall the LORD go forth, and fight against those nations, as when he fought in the day of battle. And his feet shall stand in that day on the mount of Olives, which is before Jerusalem on the east, and the mount of Olives shall split in the middle thereof toward the east and toward the west, and there shall be a very great valley; and half of the mountain shall remove toward the north, and half of it toward the south. And you shall flee to the valley of the mountains; for the valley of the mountains shall reach to Azal: yes, you shall flee, like as you fled from before the earthquake in the days of Uzziah king of Judah: <u>and the LORD my God shall come, and all the saints with you</u>. And it shall come to pass in that day, that the light shall not be clear, nor dark: But it shall be one day which shall be known to the LORD, not day, nor night: but it shall come to pass, that at evening time it shall be light. . . . And the LORD shall be king over all the earth: in that day shall there be one LORD, and his name one. . . . And this shall be the **plague** with which the LORD will smite all the people that have fought against Jerusalem; **Their flesh shall consume away while they stand on their feet, and their eyes shall consume away in their holes, and their tongue shall consume away in**

their mouth. And it shall come to pass in that day, that a great tumult from the LORD shall be among them; and they shall lay hold every one on the hand of his neighbor, and his hand shall rise up against the hand of his neighbor. And Judah also shall fight at Jerusalem; and the wealth of all the heathen round about shall be gathered together, gold, and silver, and apparel, in great abundance. And so shall be the plague of the horse, of the mule, of the camel, and of the ass, and of all the beasts that shall be in these tents, as this plague. (Zech. 14:1-15 edited)

The saints shall be resurrected and raptured and shall come with Jesus to Jerusalem to fight on behalf of Israel. Jesus will stand on the Mount of Olives, and an earthquake will split it so that Jews can escape the city safely. This *"plague"* is similar to the results of an atomic bomb, but God could use a different method.

Order and Timing of Seals, Trumpets and Vials

John described these things in an orderly fashion. The first group of four of each object is a distinct grouping. With understanding their groupings and timings, the following order can be made:

Seal #1 (Conquering white horse - 9/11/01 to present)
Seal #2 (Red war horse of Islam; from 9/11/01 to present)
Seal #3 (Black horse of economic ruin; from Sept. 2008 to present)
Seal #4 (Pale horse of death; from 9/11/01 to present)
   Great Tribulation begins 4/6/09 (counting backwards 1,260 days
   from calculated date of Christ's return on September 16, 2012)
Trumpets and Vials #1-4 (1/3 of trees, seas, rivers are spoiled)
Vial #5 (Darkness/Pain) and Trumpet #5 ('Locusts' for 5 months)
Trumpet and Vial #6 (Armegeddon War 1 1/2 years)
Seal #5 (Great Tribulation Martyrs during Armegeddon War)
Seal #6 (? 09/15/2012)
Vial #7 (09/16/2012)
Seals #7 (09/16/2012)
Trumpet #7 (09/16/2012)

Summary

Though there are seven each of the seals, trumpets and vials; the first group of four of each object is a distinct grouping. The 7 seals are global in their impact, with the first four seals before the Great Tribulation and the three remaining seals at the end. The 7 vials are poured out on Babylon (Islam) and those who worship the beast, while the 7 trumpets are experienced by the rest of the world. The first four trumpets and vials parallel each other as they make a distinction between those who worship the Beast of Islam, and those who do not, just as God made a distinction between the Egyptians and the Hebrews during the ten plagues. The trumpets and vials are not done in succession, but in tandem. The 7th seal, the 7th vial, and the 7th trumpet are simultaneous, culminating in King Jesus' return to reign and lead His army to victory.

The seven seals are opened by the "*Lamb who was slain*" who purchased the right to do so in preparation to retrieve His Bride. Israel became a nation again, and we have divided its land. The Lamb of God has determined it is time to redeem and judge the earth, and the first four seals wake up the people of the earth to get ready for its judgment (Joel 2 and Rev. 5). Al Qaeda demonstrated to the the world what damage it could do without nukes on 9/11/01 (white horse). By that act Muslim terrorists have "*removed peace from the earth*" and have continued killing (red horse). Exactly seven years later the US entered secret negotiations to divide Jerusalem, and a devastating hurricane and economic ruin (black horse) followed a few days later. Currently Islam constitutes one fourth of the world population, and has a majority in one fourth of the world's countries, where it exercises its power to kill through war and famine (pale horse).

God will start the Great Tribulation clock as He sees fit; possibly with events in heaven unseen by us (Michael's release of Satan; sealing of the 144,000), or with events seen and heard by the world (angel proclaiming gospel and/or Antichrist's deity declaration). The destruction of the great city Babylon (Mecca with its port, Jeddeh) will occur within a year of its angelic announcement. With the Saudis out of the way, Iran (threatening blockade of the Straits of Hormuz or nuclear war) will then require all people to wear a mark of allegiance to Islam on their arm or forehead in order to buy or sell (international monetary standard of the 'gold dinar'). Muslims will eventually behead those who refuse the mark. The third angelic announcement is if anyone worships the Beast or takes its mark, he will also experience God's wrath.

It is unclear when in the first two years of the Great Tribulation these sets of four will occur, or how much time is allotted to each or between each. They begin after 144,000 have been sealed, but sometime before March 2011.

First Four Trumpets (upon world)	First Four Vials (upon Babylon)
1st All grass burnt; 1/3 trees	1st Sores upon worshipers of Beast
2nd 1/3 sea, sea-life & ships	2nd Sea to blood; all sea-life dies
3rd 1/3 rivers; & bitter waters	3rd All rivers and fountains to blood
4th 1/3 of sun, moon & stars	4th Use sun to scorch men with fire

3/26/2011-8/23/2011 (prelude to Armegeddon)

    5th Chemical war with helicopters   5th Painful sores & darkness

8/23/2011-9/16/2012 (Armegeddon War) [5th seal during Armegeddon War]

    6th Chemical/Fire tanks   6th Dry Euphrates for Shia armies

    [6th seal]
9/16/2012 (Day of the LORD) 7th Seal and Vial and Trumpet

The 6th seal is broken within a few hours of the day of the Lord. The 7th vial will be poured out over Babylon (Islam) completing God's wrath upon them, and the 7th seal and the 7th trumpet over the world as voices, lightning, thunder, hail, and a great earthquake are experienced around the globe. The sun will be dark and the moon look like blood, but the brightness of Christ's coming will illuminate the world. Jesus will bring the resurrected saints with Him and collect His living saints en route to Jerusalem where we will all fight for Israel and be victorious over the Antichrist and all nations gathered against Israel.

Thus said the LORD, Let not the wise man glory in his wisdom, neither let the mighty man glory in his might, let not the rich man glory in his riches: But let him that glories glory in this, that he understands and knows me, that I am the LORD which exercise loving kindness, judgment, and righteousness, in the earth: for in these things I delight, said the LORD. (Jeremiah 9:23-24)

It's time to get to know the LORD and to understand His time of grace will soon end in a period of judgment. God will fulfill His Word. Jesus will return to judge the wicked and to reward His saints who have been longing to see Him. Make sure you're in the latter group.

Great Tribulation Time-line of Revelation

Eve Clarity © 04/02/2009

Seals	1 2 3 4				5 6 7
Angels (announce)	1 2 3				(reap) 4-6 7
Trumpets (world)		1 2 3 4	5	6	7
Vials (Babylon)		1 2 3 4	5	6	7
Woes			1	2	3

Wake up	<<<	1,260 days = 42(30)	5 m locusts =	3.5(360)	>>>
9/11/01	4/06/09		3/26/11	8/23/11	9/16/12
		2 years, 1/3 less trees, sea, water, and light in sky	locusts	1 yr 1 m 1 d Armegeddon Kills 1/3 world	

www.ingramcontent.com/pod-product-compliance
Lightning Source LLC
Chambersburg PA
CBHW060950050426
42337CB00052B/3487